How To Study The Bible

Applying The Proper Methods For Studying And Understanding The Scriptures

Dr. Joseph R. Rogers, Sr.

Dedication

Once again, the Lord has graced me the privilege to share with the body of Christ another vehicle of insight.

I count it an honor to be able to be used of the Lord to help those who are committed to learning and understanding the bible.

This tool will help shed some light on reading, ingesting, digesting and applying the Scriptures.

It is with humble and gracious honor that I dedicate this writing to you and it is my prayer that it will assist you in your quest for scriptural understanding. The Lord commands that we study to show ourselves approved unto Him, a workman that needed not to be ashamed, rightly dividing the word of true.

As you read this short work, I ask you to open up your heart and mind and allow the Holy Spirit to guide you in the pathway of truth and righteousness.

Once you have a working knowledge of the Scripture you will able to deal with the cunning devices of the Devil and learn how to grow in grace and the knowledge of the Lord.

In conclusion, it is my prayer that after ingesting this rich work that you will be on your way of walking in the Lord's destined plan for your life.

Be Blessed,

Table of Contents

Introduction

My brothers and sisters, if there is one critical thing that all believers must understand it is obtaining a wholesome biblical understanding of the Scriptures. The Scriptures is the believer's only lifeline.

This very fact affirms what The Apostle Paul was conveying to his son in ministry Timothy when he said, **"Study to shew thyself approved unto God, a workman that needed not be ashamed, rightly dividing the word of truth". (2 Timothy 2:15).**

Not only will the believer's lack spiritual growth and development; the sinner will only be held in darkness by the Devil, if the message of the gospel is not bought to the light. The Scriptures says, **"If our gospel be hid; it be hid for those who are lost"**.

The purpose of this work is to present basic Bible **principles** and **methods** for proper study. We will consider **proper attitudes** in study, Bible **inspiration, a comparison of the old and new laws, and the danger of following human laws and authority instead of Scripture.**

Finally, we will give some suggestions about the **proper use** of some helps such as **translations, concordance**, and **cross-references**. One of the critical areas of understanding the bible is:

*To Whom Was The Text Directed!

*The Time And Date Of The Writing!

*The Now Day Application!

So, as we **delve** into this awesome study let us come in with **an open mind and heart;** with our spiritual thinking cap on ready to understand so that we grow in grace and in the knowledge of our Lord and Savior Jesus Christ.

Blessing And Peace,

Dr. Joseph R. Rogers, Sr., Pastor/Teacher

I. Proper Attitudes in Study

As the priest Ezra, *"prepared his heart to seek the law of the Lord"* (Ezra 7:10), so must you and me. One of the most critical elements in understanding the bible is to, being with having the right attitude.

Always read the bible with the **attitude (approach, mind-set, viewpoint, or posture)** understanding that this is God speaking directly to you; therefore, I must listen attentively and be willing to accept what I read and be willing to apply what I have read without reservation.

It is when we **ingest, digest and process** the word of God within its proper context that we will develop properly and continue to mature in the will or things of the Lord.

Never view the bible as just a book. The bible is life! An when you and I approach this learning process with commitment and determination, it will be better equipped you to do the Lord's will for your life.

In this process there are some things that you must be willing to do/follow:

A. Study To:

1: Obey God and grow in His service

Joshua 1:8 - Success in pleasing God requires obedience. To obey, we must meditate on God's word day and night. Frequent and regular study is required. The more you associate yourself with something, the more acquainted you will become with it (practice makes perfect).

1 Peter 2:2 - Can a baby grow without nourishment? No, and neither can Christians grow without Bible study. Do you long for the word like a baby longs for milk? If we neglect to attend assemblies or to study at home we will shorten, hamper and take off course of developmental process,

(See also 2 Tim. 2:15; Rom. 10:17; Matt. 4:4; John 6:44,45; 2 Peter 1:12-15.)

2: To void error and false teaching

Hosea 4:6 - God's people were destroyed for lack of knowledge. Many Christians and congregations have been led astray by error and false teaching. To avoid this, we must put teachers to the test (1 John 4:1,6).

The Devil is slick, cunning and a trickster when it comes to explaining the Word of God. You must understand that this is his purpose—to steal, kill and to destroy! We cannot defense ourselves against these if our knowledge of the bible is elementary. (We must know God's word (Gal. 1:8, 9).

Acts 17:11 - The Bereans distinguished truth from error because they studied the word. To imitate their example, we must study "daily."

(See also Matt. 22:29; 15:14; Prov. 2:1-20; Rom. 10:1-3.)

3: Teach others

Deuteronomy 6:6-9 - Parents should teach their children diligently throughout the day. This requires us to first have God's word in our own hearts. How can we teach what we do not know?

Hebrews 5:12 - The time comes when we ought to be teachers, but these had not studied so they needed others to teach them! There is no excuse for Christians who do not study. Teachers know they need to study.

(See also 2 Tim. 2:2; 1 Tim. 1:7; 1 Peter 3:15; Col. 3:16; Rom. 15:14.)

4: Express love for God and His word

Psalm 1:2; 119:47,48,97-99 - One who delights in God's word will meditate on it day and night. The time we spend thinking about God's word indicates how much we love Him.

Those who truly love Him will not complain about "having to go" to worship services or prepare for Bible classes. (See Psalm 19:7-11.)

John 14:15 - If we love God, we keep His commands (cf. 1 John 5:3). But obedience requires knowledge. So those who love God must study His word.

5. With an Open Mind & a Love for Truth

We must strive to learn truth and obey it regardless of the consequences. Seek it even if you disagree with what you have believed or have been taught in the past and always be willing to change.

Acts 17:11 - The Bereans were also noble because they received the word with readiness of mind - minds open to truth.

Matthew 5:6 - Hunger and thirst after righteousness.

It is as fact that some misunderstand truth because they close their hearts, eyes, and ears. They enjoy practices or have prejudices contrary to what God teaches. They have motives for rejecting Bible teaching, so they satisfy their own minds that it is not true.

If we do not have a burning desire for truth, God will not force us to accept the truth. He will let us be lost (cf. 2 Thess. 2:10-12; 2 Tim. 4:2-4; John 3:19-21).

(See also 2 Cor. 13:5; 1 Thess. 5:21,22; Prov. 18:13; 23:23; 15:10; Luke 8:15; 1 Sam. 3:9,10.)

B. Respect the Bible as Being Verbally & Infallibly Inspired.

If a person doubts that the Bible is God's infallible word, he/she is much more likely to disagree or reject it. I have found that some people believe that man wrote the bible without the aid of the Holy Spirit.

The bible teaches and shows us that these persons **were inspired by/of God** as they wrote what. The Lord instructed them to write. It covers over **1600 years**, using approximately **forty (40) different human writers**, in approximately **three (3) languages**.

It is without question that the BIBLE is the words of the Creator, Father and **'Finite God'** of the universe and He that used men/women to pen it on paper. Therefore...etc.

a. **The Bible is from God:**

2 Timothy 3:16,17 - All scripture is inspired by God to teach us and provide us to all good works.

1 Thessalonians 2:13 - It is the word of God not of men (cf. Gal. 1:11,12).

1 Corinthians 14:37 - Paul wrote the commands of the Lord. To reject any command is to reject the will of God.

(See also Eph. 3:3-5; Luke 10:16; 2 Peter 1:20,21.)

b. The Bible is verbally inspired:

Some people believe that God just gave the inspired men ideas, then let them explain them as they saw fit. This belief leaves room for 'error' in the way the men expressed the ideas.

"Verbal Inspiration" means that every word written by the inspired writers was exactly the word God wanted.

Deuteronomy 18:18,19 - God put His words in the prophet's mouth, so the prophet spoke (or wrote) the very words chosen by God Himself.

(See 1 Cor. 2:3-5; Matt. 10:19,20; 2 Sam. 23:1,2; Ex. 24:3,4,7; Isa. 51:l6; Jer. 1:5-9.)

c. The Bible is infallible:

The message of the inspired writers cannot possibly be wrong because God does not make mistakes and does not contradict (disagree with) Himself

Psalm 119:128 - God's word is always true and right.

Titus 1:2 - God cannot lie or be wrong.

St. Matthew 22:32; Galatians 3:16 - The Scriptures are so accurate that we can rely even on the tense of the verbs and the plurality or singularity of words. We should approach the Bible with faith that every word is exactly right and true; otherwise we may reject its teaching.

(Cf. John 17:17; Psalm 33:4; 19:8; 147:4,5; Rom. 3:4; Job 37:16; Num. 23:19; Heb. 6:18; Deut. 18:20-22).

d. The Bible Can Be Understood:

Some believe that the Bible can be understood only by specially-trained **preachers or teacher**, but not by the average person. As a result, they approach the Bible convinced they will never understand it. In doing so they put forth only a **half-hearted effort** to try to comprehend what is said.

St. Mark 12:37; Acts 17:11 - Inspired teachings were addressed to the common people, not to some special elite group. (See also Gal. 1:2; 1 Thess. 1:1; 5:27; 2 Peter 1:1; Rev. 1:4.)

St. Mark 7:14 - Jesus required everyone among the great crowds of people to understand His teaching.

2 Timothy 3:16,17 - The Scriptures are profitable to teach and provide to all good works. What profit would they be if we could not understand?

People were **expected to understand** the written word (Eph. 5:17). Instead of just **accepting whatever preachers say**, people should use the scriptures to check out the teachers (Acts 11:17).

(See also 1 Cor. 14:33; Eph. 3:3-5; Isa. 55:11; 35:8; John 20:30,31; 8:32; Prov. 2:1-12; Psalm 19:7ff; 119:105; Col. 1:9-11; 2 Peter 3:15,16.)

Again, approach the bible as your road map to God's destiny for your life and the necessity of comprehending what it is conveying to you. If you approach it with that attitude, the

Holy Spirit will open up your understanding—He is the inspirer and interpreter!

II: Principles of Bible Authority

St. Luke 8:18 warns us to **take heed how we hear**. Likewise, we must take **heed how we study the Bible**. To know how to study, we must understand the principles God uses to teach us.

These principles are not hidden, or hard to understand but only by a few people. Even though it is a fact that God have **anointed teachers** to teacher the His Word; yet these principles can be understood by anyone who has the right attitude, motive and desire.

Teacher are appointed and anointed to help clarify the scripture even more as we study together in group settings. Teacher are not designed to be **show offs, put downers and lifted in selfish pride because of their abilities,** but **a blessing** to the body of Christ and the local church,

There are some things that God has **revealed to us** in His principles.

A. God's Commands for Us Today Are Revealed in the New Testament

(*Note: The Old Testament laws came from God even though some of the application for the New Testament believers are applied in a different way).

Hebrews 10:9, 10 - Because the first covenant (will) did not provide complete forgiveness of sins (v3, 4), Jesus took it away and established the second covenant.

Colossians 2:14, 16 - Jesus' death blotted out the old law, so we are not bound by such regulations as unclean meats, feast days, and the Sabbath.

Galatians 3:24,25 - The law was a schoolmaster to bring us to Christ. Now we are no longer under the schoolmaster.

a. Understand it from this illustration:

Formerly our forefathers were under the laws of Great Britain then under the Articles of Confederation. Now that the **Constitution** has come, those previous legal systems are no longer totally binding. So today, anyone who seeks to bind the Law of Moses has fallen from grace (Gal. 5:1-4).

Many Old Testament practices are **not applicable for the New Testament believer**: Animal Sacrifices, Levitical Priesthood, Seventh-Day Sabbath, Physical Circumcision, Feast Days... etc.

(See also Rom. 7:1-7; Eph. 2:11-18; Heb. 8:6-13; 9:15-20; 7:11-25; Jer. 31:31-34.)

Understand it for this perspective; the Old Testament Scriptures were written for **our learning** (Rom. 15:4; 1 Cor. 10:6, 11). The Old Testament can **help us understand the totality of God's person, character and integrity**. But keep in mind that we cannot please **God based upon our works**, even though **work proves that we have faith in Jesus Christ**.

b. **History**:

The Old Testament records the Creation (Gen. 1 & 2), and God's dealings with man until the coming of Jesus. Many New Testament passages assume we believe **these historical records** (Acts 7; Heb. 11; etc.). Without these records there would be a 'gap' in our studies and this would affect our complete understand of who God The Father really is.

c. **Evidence**:

The Old Testament provides abundant evidence for the existence of God, the inspiration of the Bible, and the Deity of Jesus. This includes:

(1) The accuracy of the Bible in history, geography, and science;

(2) Fulfilled prophecy (see John 5:39; Acts 3:24);

(3) The unity of the Bible - harmony between Old Testament and New Testament.

Even though in past years there had been **doubt** as to the existence of some **biblical artifacts**; yet today **'evidence'** has proved that the historical perspective of God is real and true. For example, the **Garden of Eden, Noah Ark, Solomon's Temple** to name a few.

d. Unchanging Principles:

Although God's laws have changed, many facts about the Universe, the nature of man, and the nature of God do not change (Heb. 13:8). For example, the Old Testament **shows** that men are tempted, often sin, and need forgiveness (Rom. 3:9-23; 1 Cor. 10:1-12). The new covenant gives clear understanding that 'grace' is in force now.

e. **Appreciation and Understanding of the New Testament**:

Old Testament prophecies help us **understand** the New Testament (cf. Isa. 53; Acts 15:14-18). Further, when New Testament **commands are the same** as the Old, that helps us understand the New even better (cf. Heb. 11).

While we should not use the Old Testament **to justify our practices (relationship) today,** neither should we **neglect to study it.** We can never fully appreciate and understand God's dealings with us unless we study the Old Testament and New Testament.

B. **In the Bible, God Uses Three Basic Methods to Reveal His Will.**

We often use various methods to communicate or teach others. It is important that we understand and accept the methods that God use to communicate to and with us.

To the contrary of some beliefs today, God uses **visions, dreams, nature** as well as **His spoken and written Word** to speak to and dialogue with His children.

a. Commands and direct statements

1 Corinthians 14:37 - Paul wrote commands of the Lord. Many other passages also mention the importance of **commands** (John 14:15,21-24; 15:14; 1 John 5:3; 2:3,4; Matt. 28:18-20).

The Bible uses commands in teaching us about such subjects as **baptism** (Acts 10:48), **love**

(Matt. 22:37-40), **the Lord's supper** (1 Cor. 11:23-25), etc. [Eph. 6:2; 1 Cor. 16:1,2]

b. Examples and illustrations

Instead of directly commanding us to do something, God sometimes tells us **indirectly by giving an instance** in which Christians acted by His guidance. We are expected to imitate or follow these examples. With these there is sometime **apprehension** to move in the Lord; yet God will always assure us that it is of Him.

1 Peter 2:21, 22 - Jesus left an example we should follow. (Phil. 2:5; Matt. 10:24,25; 16:24; 1 John 2:6)

Philippians 3:17; 4:9 - Imitate Paul's example as a pattern. Do the things seen in him as well as things heard from him. (1 Cor. 11:1; 1

Tim. 1:16; 1 Cor. 4:16; 2 Thess. 3:7,9; 2 Tim. 3:10; Heb. 6:12)

Acts 15:5-11 - Peter taught others to imitate his example in teaching Gentiles.

Specifically, we can learn much about salvation from examples of conversion in the book of Acts. Still other Bible examples teach us about:

Faith (Heb. 11:1-12:4; James 5:10,11),

The action of baptism (Acts 8:35-39),

The day for the Lord's supper (Acts 20:7), and

Elders (Acts 14:23). (Cf. 1 Cor. 10:1-12; Heb. 4:11; 2 Peter 2:6; Luke 10:30-37.)

c. Logical necessary conclusions ("necessary inferences which are [conclusions, conjecture]" or "Scriptural reasoning"

Some truths are not directly or expressly stated yet they necessarily follow as **a logical consequence of what is stated**. For example, if I tell you my birthday, you can determine my age.

Acts 17:1-3 - Paul's custom was to reason from the Scriptures to convince Jews that Jesus was Christ, yet the prophecies he used did not directly state the conclusion. [Acts 2:22-36; 18:4,19; 19:8,9; 28:23; Isa. 1:18; 1 Peter 3:15]

Matthew 19:3-9 - Jesus used God's statement about marriage between two people to reach an unstated conclusion that **divorce** (not for fornication) displeases God and remarriage afterwards is adultery.

Hebrews 7:11-18 - The Old Testament allowed priests only of the tribe of Levi, but it predicted a priest of the tribe of Judah. The necessary conclusion was that the law would change. (For other examples see Acts 11:1-18; 15:6-21; Gal. 3:10-12; 1 Cor. 15:12-19; Matt. 22:23-32; 21:28-46; 22:41-46.)

All Biblical parables required reasoning to **understand** the implied lesson (Matt. 16:5-12; 25:14-30; Mark 4:33,34; etc.)

Mature Christians must use wisdom to apply the principles of God's word to specific situations (Heb. 5:14). As in a math problem, we *"add up"* the information given **to reach a conclusion**.

Note: (Only Divine Authority, not Human Authority, Is Acceptable).

When a **practice** does not include in what God has authorized in His Word we should not participate in it. Remember, the Scriptures provide us to every good work. What about 'works' it does not provide? Consider the Bible teaching:

*The Bible teaching about wisdom

Isaiah 55:8,9 - God's thoughts and ways are so different from ours - so completely higher than ours - that we cannot possibly know what He wants without **revelation**. [Luke 16:15]

Jeremiah 10:23 - Man is not wise enough to direct his paths without Divine guidance.

Proverbs 14:12 - Ways that seem right to us, result in death. This is why we must not follow human wisdom in religion.

1 Corinthians 1:21-24; 2:5 - Human wisdom leads men to reject God's will. We must follow God's wisdom, but only when it is completely revealed in the Scriptures.

Do not add to nor take from God's word (Rev. 22:18, 19). To practice things not found in the word is to follow human wisdom. This displeases God. [Deut. 4:2; 12:32; Prov. 30:6]

*The Bible teaching about worship

St. John 4:23,24 - Worship God in spirit and truth. God's word is truth (John 17:17) and provides us with all truth (John 16:13). Hence, we must not worship in any way not revealed in God's word.

St. Matthew 15:9,13 - Worship is vain (worthless) when based on **human doctrines**. If God did not originate it, man did. Since the Bible includes everything God revealed, practices not revealed in the Bible must be human in origin and therefore vain.

Worship is intended to **please and glorify God**. We respect Him by doing what He says. To do what **men say** is to respect human wisdom, not God's wisdom. Note the example in Lev. 10:1-3.

*The Bible teaching about love

St. Matthew 22:37 - The greatest command is to love God completely. Love leads us to obey God's commands (John 14:15; 1 John 5:3). But all His commands are in the Bible. Hence, love teaches us to do only what we find in the Bible. To follow human doctrines shows love, not for God, but for men.

People often defend their practices by saying "I think it's beautiful," or "We're satisfied with it." But this is irrelevant when we are serving God. Does a man show love for his wife by getting her a power tool for her birthday because he wants it? We serve God by offering what HE likes, and that is completely revealed in the Bible.

*The Bible teaching about faith

We cannot please God without faith (Heb. 11:6). But we must walk by faith (2 Cor. 5:7). Faith is the way of walking or living that must be demonstrated in action. [Gal. 2:20; 5:6; James 2:14-26; Heb. 11]

Romans 10:17 - Faith comes by hearing God's word. The only way to know God's will is by what He has revealed. To practice things not revealed is to fail to walk by faith.

Proverbs 3:5,6 - If we trust in the Lord, we will let Him direct our paths. We do not lean on our own understanding. Human wisdom is not adequate to determine God's will.

If a man has complete faith in his doctor and not in himself, would he reject the doctor's prescription and follow his own? No, that shows faith in self instead of the doctor.

The teachings that we follow are a demonstration of **whom we trust**. To practice things not found in the Bible is to trust human wisdom instead of God's.

*The Bible teaching about authority

2 John 9 - Whoever does not abide in Jesus' teaching does not have God. To have God, we must abide in the teaching. To practice things not found in Jesus' teaching would separate us from Him.

Galatians 1:8,9 - Any man is accursed if he preaches a gospel that differs from what inspired men taught in the first century.

God never intended for His word to itemize everything we should not practice. Instead He tells us what **He DOES want**. Then **He forbids** our practicing things He has not authorized.

Instead of asking "Where does God forbid this act?" we ought to ask, "Where does God tell us to do this act?" If an act is not included in what He said to do, we should leave it alone.

(Col. 3:17; 1 Peter 4:11; 1 Cor. 4:6; 2 Cor. 10:18; Rom. 10:1-3; Col. 2:8]

E. God May Teach in General or Specific Terms.

Our practices must fit the definition or fall within the meaning of the instructions God has given. However, people sometimes misunderstand

Scripture because they fail to distinguish **specific language from general language.**

*A statement of the principle:

*Specific authority:

God has told us not to practice things that do not fit the meaning of His instructions. So, when He wants us to do a thing in a particular way, He instructs us by choosing words that are **specific or narrow (limited, restricted, exclusive)** in their meaning. If we then do things differently, outside the limits of the meaning of the terms He uses, we displease Him.

*General authority:

When God wants to leave men free to choose from several alternative ways of doing a thing, He instructs us with words that are more **general or broad** (inclusive, comprehensive, all-encompassing) in their meaning. We still must do only what fits the instruction, but we are free to choose any of the various alternatives that fit. Any such choice would be acceptable because we would still be doing what God said.

*Applications of the Principle

Noah and the ark - Gen. 6:14

God told Noah to make an ark of gopher wood. Metal, pine, walnut, etc., do not fit the definition of gopher wood. They constitute different kinds of materials. God did not expressly say not to use them, but He excluded them by saying "gopher wood" and remaining silent about metal, pine, etc.

Had God wanted to leave Noah free to use any kind of material, He could simply have said to make an ark, and specified no material at all. Then Noah could have chosen any kind of material and He would still have been obeying God. But when God specified the material, the use of any other material would have been disobedience.

On the other hand, there are many things a person can do that would fit the definition of "making" an ark. He might use a hammer and saw, or pegs and glue. None of these things are specifically mentioned, but they would have been acceptable because, while using them, Noah would still be doing what God said to do.

*Going to preach the gospel - Mark 16:15

God said to go preach the gospel to every creature. If we preach man-made doctrines, we are not preaching the gospel. Therefore, to preach them is unacceptable.

On the other hand, there are many ways a person might "go" into all the world. He might walk, ride a donkey, car, chariot, plane, etc. These things may not be specifically mentioned, but any or all of them would be acceptable because they fit the definition of "going".

In the same way, there are many things a person could do that would constitute preaching the gospel. He might speak to a group of people, write them a letter, divide them up into classes, speak over radio or TV or write on a blackboard or overhead projector. All such would fit the meaning of what God said to do.

III. Rules For Scripture Conformation

A. Consider Other Passages on the Same Subject.

(Truth on a subject is determined by "adding up" **all pertinent passages)**

Acts 3:22,23 - Hearken to all things Jesus spoke. Bible study is not like a cafeteria where you take what you want and leave the rest.

St. Matthew 4:4,7 - Live by every word from God's mouth. For example, Jesus showed that the devil has misused one passage by considering another passage.

St. John 17:17; 1 Corinthians 14:33 - God's word is truth. He is not the author of confusion. Truth does not contradict itself.

Never **"interpret"** a passage in a way that contradicts other passages. Conclusions should harmonize with all that God has spoken.

(Rev. 22:18, 19; Acts 20:20,27; Matt. 28:20; 12:25,26; James 2:10; 2 Tim. 3:16,17; 1 Cor. 1:10,13]

*Some applications

The pattern of salvation and worship is not entirely revealed in one passage. We must study many passages and take the whole pattern.

So, some members of the Lord's church emphasize the command to be **baptized**, then apparently ignore verses that require **a faithful life, attendance**, etc.

B. Consider Context and Background.

By "Context" means the verses surrounding the one being studied, especially verses on the same subject.

By "Background" we mean who is speaking, to whom they speak, etc. These are just a particular form of considering all the Bible says.

Some specific benefits of considering context and background:

**Word meanings:

Words may have different meanings in different contexts. We learn the correct meaning by how the word is used.

Acts 20:17, 28 shows that the "**elders**" (v17) are "**bishops**" or "**overseers**" (v28). Hence, both terms refer to the same work or office.

**Further explanation:

When a verse confuses us, other statements nearby may clarify the meaning.

Acts 16:31-34 - Some people claim v31 means we are saved by "faith only," and that **grace and baptism** has no part. But v32-34 shows that only part of the gospel had been taught.

**Proper application:

Often a statement can best be understood by considering how it is applied in context.

Romans 7:1-7 - We have been discharged from the law, but what law does this mean? It included, "Thou shalt not covet" (v7) - one of the Ten Commands. Hence, the law that we are freed from, includes the Ten Commands that we must follow.

**The speaker:

Every Bible word is infallible, but sometimes it infallibly records the sins or lies of fallible people.

Psalm 14:1 quotes "There is no God." But who says this? The fool says it. The Bible accurately records, not that the statement is true, but that foolish people truly do say it.

50

Job 2:9 says "Curse God and die." But who says this? Job's wife said it and was immediately rebuked by Job.

To understand the Bible properly we must realize that sometimes it accurately records the fact that fallible people do or say sinful things.

The people addressed, when and where:

Not all instructions in the Bible - not even all that God spoke - are intended for us to obey.

Genesis 6:13,14 - God told Noah to build an ark. Must we build one?

Genesis 22:1,2 - God told Abraham to sacrifice his son. Must we slay ours?

St. Luke 23:39-43 - Jesus said the thief on the cross would be in Paradise, so some conclude we today can be saved without baptism.

But the man Jesus addressed lived under the Old Testament before Jesus died to remove it (Heb. 9:16,17; Col. 2:14). This no more applies today than the command to Noah to build the ark or the command to Abraham to slay his son.

C. Define the Meaning of the Words.

The Bible is verbally inspired - each word is from God (see previous notes). The message is revealed in words, and we understand it only when we understand the words.

Words are sometimes used today in ways that completely differ from the meaning in the

Bible. Consider such words as the following: **saint, church, bishop, Christian, etc.**

The word *"baptism"* is defined today as sprinkling, pouring, or immersion, but in the Bible, it means immersion (Rom. 6:4; Acts 8:38, 39).

Dictionaries may help, but the best way to learn Bible words is to study them by the means already discussed: context and parallel passages.

IV: Tools & Suggested Procedures for Bible Study

Having completed our study of requirements for Bible study, we will now offer some helps and suggested methods of applying these principles. These ideas harmonize with the principles we have learned, but other approaches may fit them too.

A. Helpful Tools for Study

***Translations:

The Bible was written in **Hebrew and Greek**, so we need translations into our language.

Since the Bible is verbally inspired, translations ought to give the exact meaning of the original words.

Unfortunately, some **modern "translations"** are too loose, emphasizing eloquent expression instead of original meaning. Other translations come from a man or a denomination, so their views may influence their work.

Seek a translation made by many men from different groups, who believe in **verbal inspiration** and who emphasize the meaning of **the original words.**

For a primary study Bible, we suggest the **King James Version, New King James Version, American Standard Version, or New American**

Standard Version. Others may be useful for comparison, but not for a main study Bible. Comparing several translations may help clarify the text.

***Cross references:

Some Bibles have **footnotes** on each verse that refer to other similar verses. From those verses you might find still others, etc. This is useful for "studying other verses on the subject."

***Concordance:

A concordance lists words in the Bible alphabetically and gives passages where each word is used. Some concordances are brief; others are more complete.

Uses of a concordance include:

(1) Finding many passages about a subject;

(2) Finding a particular verse if you know one or two words in it;

(3) Determining the meaning of a word by studying verses where it is used.

***Other helps:

The following helps may be useful, but remember they are written by fallible humans who can be wrong.

*Bible dictionaries and encyclopedias are descriptions, listed alphabetically, of Bible people, places, things, and events. Emphasis is on history and geography. Do *not* expect detailed definitions or discussions of doctrinal matters.

*Word study helps include "expository dictionaries" and lexicons. These actually define Bible words. You look up the English word in an expository dictionary, but you must know the Greek or Hebrew alphabet to use a lexicon. Be careful with these books if you have no training in the original languages.

*Commentaries are verse-by-verse explanations of the Bible text.
Be especially careful because the authors' beliefs may contradict Scripture. If you use commentaries, study several to get alternative views, consider the *reasons* the author gives for his view, and always let the Bible be your final authority.

B. Suggested Procedures for Bible Study

Too many people do not study the Bible in an **organized way**, and too many depend on

others to study for them. It may not be wrong to use someone else's material to guide us in a study, yet some members cannot study for themselves.

The following suggestions are designed to help you start with just a few basic Bible study tools and study a Bible passage or subject for yourself.

They are general guidelines that may be abbreviated or modified in some cases. But they should be helpful in learning God's word.

(Suggested procedure for studying a Bible passage)

Suppose you have a particular section of Scripture you want to study: a verse, chapter, section, or even a whole book. The following procedure will help you use the principles we have learned.

1. Study the general background of the book of the Bible. Who wrote it? What do you know about the author? To whom was it written, and what do you know about these people? When was it written and under what circumstances? You may learn this information from reading the book itself (see next step) or by using cross-references, concordances, etc.

2. Read the passage in context. You may need to read the whole book. Understand the theme of the book, and list the main subjects discussed.

3. Study the particular passage section by section. Examine each paragraph, each verse, each phrase, and even each word. Define key words using context, parallel passages, other translations, and dictionaries. Study other passages on the subject (use cross references and concordance).

Ask yourself questions about what the passage does and does not mean and consider alternative views. Search for evidence till you can answer your questions, prove what view is correct, and explain the meaning in your own words.

Think of examples or illustrations to help explain the passage. Make specific applications to your own life and the lives of others. Write careful notes throughout your study and save your notes for future reference.

(Suggested procedure for studying a Bible subject)

1. Select and define the topic. Write it as precisely as you can in a few statements or questions. Revise if necessary as you proceed.

2. Jot down everything you think you know about the topic: Passages, main points, illustrations, applications, etc.

3. List the important words related to the topic. You will use these to find pertinent passages in the concordance. Be sure to define them as you proceed.

4. List the important passages. Use memory, concordance, cross references, etc.

5. Study each passage using the methods previously described for passages. Ask questions, draw conclusions, make applications, think of illustrations.

6. Organize the material. Divide your topic logically into its major divisions and sub-divisions. Classify each item of information under the appropriate sub-division. (If you cannot do this, you probably need to study more to understand the material better.)

Again, take careful notes at each step. You may want to write a final outline or summary of the material, especially if it is to be taught to others. Save your notes for future study.

V. Conclusion

God's word not only teaches **why we should study**, but it also teaches us **how to study**. We have no good excuse for not studying and learning God's word.

Our eternal destiny depends upon our understanding of **God's destiny** for us—that is, God desire is that none should perish, but that all would come to know the knowledge of the truth (scriptures).

When you and I refuse to dig into the Scripture we open ourselves to **false doctrines** and **err**. It is a known fact that if we do not clearly understand of the Scriptures; this will lead us to **disobeying God** and eventually **falling into sin.**

Even though we are tired sometimes for the daily **hustle** and **bustle** of life; we must never forget to feed our **spirit man.** If you do not feed our **spirit man** he will suffer from **lack of nutrients,** which leads to **spiritual death**!

When studying the Scriptures always read with an open mind; that is to obtain knowledge or insights and never to try to find scriptures that agrees with your conviction or thinking.

Study to be matured in the things of God!

Joseph R. Rogers, Sr., D. Min

VI. The Author's Contact Information And Other Works

A. Mailing Address:

1313 Ujamaa Drive, Raleigh, NC 27610

B. Email Address:

jroger3420@aol.com,

jrrphila1428@aol.com

C. Websites:

http://gpcminc.cwwsites.com, **lulu.com,**

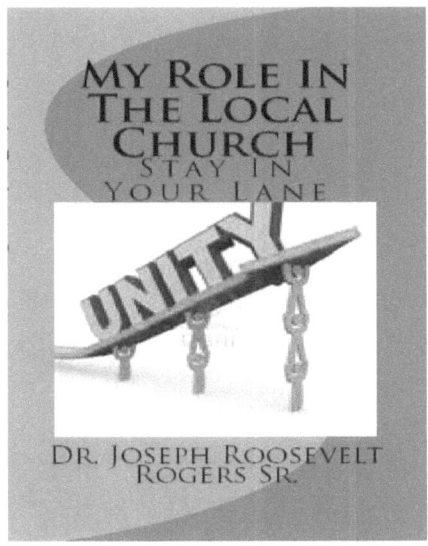

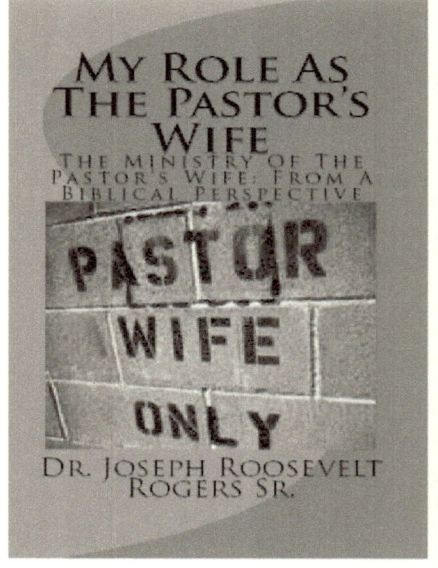

DIVORCE GOD'S WAY (FROM A BIBLICAL PERSPECTIVE)

Trust God..Pick Up The
Pieces..And Move Forward

Dr. Joseph R. Rogers Sr.

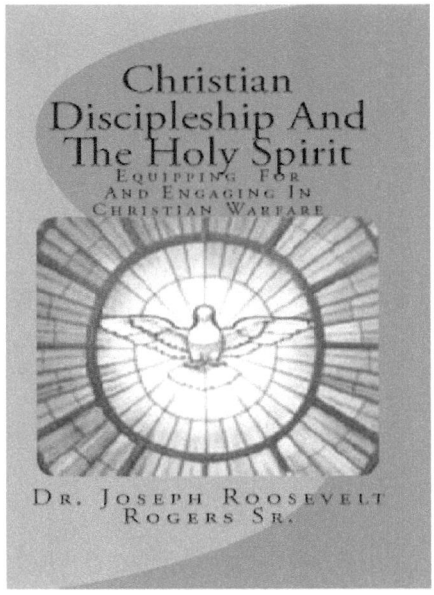

Christian
Discipleship And
The Holy Spirit
Equipping For
And Engaging In
Christian Warfare

Dr. Joseph Roosevelt
Rogers Sr.

MARRIAGE GOD'S WAY
"KEEP THE FIRE BURNING"

DR. JOSEPH R. ROGERS, SR.

CHURCH LEADERSHIP
THE PASTOR AND THE DEACON

DR. JOSEPH R. ROGERS SR.

VII. Notes

Notes Con't.

VIII. Tidbits To The Bible Student

1. Always remember that the The Bible is the Christian handbook for life.

2. Always remember that The Bible contains God's Word to man.

3. Always remember that The Bible is God's instructions for victorious living.

4. Always remember that reading and studying the Bible is an important essential in spiritual development.

5. Always set aside time for Bible ingestion, digestion for future application.

6. Always remember to read The Bible as God speaking directly to you.

7. Always remember to never take The Bible out of its context.

8. Always remember that The Bible is for application and not interpretation.

9. Always remember that The Bible is your lamp and light—follow it!

10. Always remember to study The Bible with an open mind and heart.

IX. Basic Rules For Studying The Bible

(Source: *Fourteen Rules for Bible Study* by F. Coulter)

1. If possible have a regular, private place for your Bible studies. Before each study ask God to give you a spirit of humility while reading His word and guide your heart to comprehending, accepting and practicing His precious truth.

2. Start with Bible verses that are easy to understand when studying on a

particular topic. Then, use these scriptures to understand harder, vaguer passages of God's word.

3. Let the Bible interpret and prove the Bible. Don't look for what YOU want to prove; look for what the Bible actually proves.

4. Seek to understand the general context of a particular Bible verse by reading the verses and chapters just before and after it. Does your understanding of a Bible passage harmonize with the rest of Scripture? Remember, the Bible DOES NOT contradict itself!

5. Study the original language (Hebrew or Greek) words and their meaning(s) behind a Bible verse. Remember,

however, that although study aids like *Strong's Exhaustive Concordance of the Bible* can be helpful, they should not be exclusively used to discover and prove what the Bible teaches.

6. ASK, what does the scripture you are studying **clearly** say?

7. ASK, what does the scripture you are studying NOT say?

8. ASK, to whom was the Bible book containing the scripture you are studying written to? Who wrote the book? Who is speaking the scripture(s) in question?

9. Seek to understand the general time frame in history when the Bible verses you are studying was written.

10. Remember that the Bible at times uses parables, allegories, symbols, poetry, metaphors and other figures of speech and literary techniques to reveal God's truth.

11. Don't bring your own personal assumptions and preconceived notions into your understanding or conclusions.

12. Base your study on scriptural knowledge that you already understand. WHAT DO YOU KNOW UP TO THIS POINT IN TIME?

13. Do not form conclusions based on partial facts or insufficient information, or the opinions and speculations of others.

14. Remember that your or anyone else's convictions, regardless of how strong they may be, don't necessarily count. GOD'S WORD is your ultimate standard and guide.

www.ingramcontent.com/pod-product-compliance
Lightning Source LLC
Chambersburg PA
CBHW021237280526
45784CB00005B/2128